The 10 Secrets

to Higher Student Achievement

James R. Garver

Design: Buse Printing

Consistent with modern usage, the editors have chosen to use data as both a plural and a singular mass noun form.

For information, address All Star Publishing, 2525 East Arizona Biltmore Circle, Suite 240, Phoenix, AZ 85016, (800) 242-3419.

All Star Publishing
First Edition 2005

Dedication

To my mother, Carolyn Garver Bickley,
who would have been so proud of this book

and to my wife, Lorie,
without whose love, collaboration, and support
it would never have been possible.

Acknowledgements

In many ways, this book is a synthesis of the best of what we know in education. I would like to thank the great researchers and thinkers of our profession for their contributions to this book and to my own professional knowledge. I especially admire Larry Lezotte whose work brings so many of the pieces together.

While research is vital, practical experience and implementation bring abstract concepts to life. I owe so much to the school systems in which I have worked and the supportive friends and colleagues who have taught me so much. Special thanks to Bill Smith, perhaps the most visionary educator I've known.

A colleague and friend, John Antonetti has shown me how to combine solid academic content with a sense of joy and fun. I would like to thank him for sharing his expertise and for writing the foreword to this book.

Linda Auman, Lorie Garver, and the incredible staff at Learning 24/7 have provided me with so many professional opportunities. You are reading this book due to their confidence and encouragement.

Finally, thanks to the wonderful teachers and administrators who have invited me into their districts to share a few of my thoughts and experiences. You shape our future every day. I salute you.

Foreword

I've had a great week-not just a great day, mind you, but a great week! It was a series of days when everything that happened made me remember and celebrate why I became a teacher. The week began with the opportunity to spend three days working with a group of exceptionally capable (and intense) educators from around the country as we processed all of the latest research in education and planned for professional learning around the ideas of lesson planning, strategic teaching, and high expectations. I continue to be amazed at the power and spiritual benefit of educators coming together to reflect and improve their practice.

As the week progressed, I encountered two teachers who were also authors. The first author is a high-profile thinker and writer in the business and science world. His name is Malcom Gladwell and his new book is entitled *Blink*. The book challenges all humans to hone and honor the "adaptive unconscious" that allows us to make hundreds of valid, instinctive decisions during the course of a day. Gladwell encourages us to shape, manage, and educate these unconscious reactions and to give them credit equal to those decisions we make after long, deliberate data collection and analyses.

The implications for the classroom are incredible. As teachers working with 25 to 35 students at a time, how many split-second decisions do we make as we interact, respond, and provide feedback to our students! The underlying premise of Gladwell's *Blink* is that these metacognitive flashes must represent the synthesis of all that we have learned and experienced in our chosen field.

This leads me to the next author I encountered in my thought provoking "power week." This author was a member of the previously-mentioned group of educators who had challenged my thinking and reinforced my passions about public education. He is the author of the book you now hold in your hand and he has ties to Malcom Gladwell that he may not realize.

As a classroom teacher, principal, administrator and college professor, Jim Garver has built a collective understanding—nay, wisdom—about teaching and learning that he imparts in this volume. *Ten Secrets* serves as that synthesis of ideas and practices that educators must make a part of their conscious planning for student achievement. Even more than that, the secrets imparted in this book serve as those whispers and internal voices that inform our instinct and allow us to make student-centered decisions as fast as our neurons can spark.

A gifted storyteller, Jim uses the power of the parable to highlight and connect us to each of the secrets of student achievement in an artful way. (My personal favorites are the stories in Secret #8.) Practical applications and translations accompany each idea and lead to insight and additional resources.

Whether you are looking for systemic growth in a school/district or looking to inform the thousands of fleeting moments that present themselves in your own classroom, I know you will find Jim Garver's *Ten Secrets* a wonderful, elegantly simple tool.

As his stories distill for us what Jim has learned about teaching, they teach us about learning.

John Antonetti
Senior Consultant
Learning 24/7

Contents

Introduction

"Pssst . . . I want to tell you a secret."

Those words certainly get our attention, don't they? Whether it's small town gossip or international espionage, we find the idea of secrets fascinating. As children or adults, the unknown contents of a wrapped present can drive us to distraction. We love to read and watch mysteries, in which secrets are withheld until the end of the story. And songwriters know the power of secrets, too. They have given us *Secret Love*, *Do You Want to Know a Secret*, *My Baby Has a Secret*, and, of course, *I Heard It Through the Grapevine*.

Secrets have been a part of commercial success as well. You may be old enough to remember that Colonel Sanders of Kentucky Fried Chicken fame was a real person and not just a character on a logo. In 1930, Harland Sanders began providing food for hungry travelers who stopped at his gas station in Corbin, Kentucky. He served the food from his own kitchen table. Eventually, he bought a small restaurant and perfected a unique method for cooking chicken. When an interstate highway threatened to bypass Corbin and end his small business, Harland Sanders, age 65 (who by now had been made a Kentucky Colonel by Governor Ruby Lafoon), devoted himself to franchising his business idea. The rest, as they say, is history (KFC Corporation, 2002).

Although he patented a new process for frying chicken, much of the Colonel's success was attributed to the unusual taste of his chicken's batter coating. He attributed the flavor to a special blend of "eleven secret herbs and spices." This catch phrase even became part of the company's advertising campaign. For years, when people met him, they would ask, "Colonel, what are those eleven secret ingredients?" All he would say is, "You can find them all in the pantry of any well-stocked kitchen."

At this point, one might ask, "What does this have to do with student achievement?"

Many of the factors that affect student achievement seem to be out of our control. Studies have shown that poverty, language acquisition, and even the education level of parents can have a profound effect on student learning and the ability to demonstrate that learning on standardized instruments (Guild & Garger, 1998). Yet, there are schools and districts that, faced with daunting demographic challenges, still succeed. In newspapers and professional journals, we read of schools in inner cities and isolated rural areas where poverty is oppressive, where there is a history of failure, where there is little financial support for education, and where students are still able to meet and exceed state standards. Then, we look at our own classrooms, scratch our heads, and wonder. How do they do it? What do those schools know that we don't? What are their secrets?

By synthesizing experience and research, this book attempts to answer those questions. You will find, however, that *The 10 Secrets to Higher Student Achievement* have much in common with the secret ingredients in Colonel Sanders' batter coating. As you read through the chapters, much of what you encounter may seem familiar. You may have heard some of these ideas in a staff development program. You may have learned about some of them in a professional publication or a graduate class. Your school may even have implemented several of them. But here's where the Colonel comes in. While these ten secrets may have familiar elements, their power comes in implementing them in combination, intentionally and consistently. Find the recipe that's right for your students, and you may find other educators asking, "What's *your* secret?"

Like many good secrets, you'll find that these are in code. They look like this:

THE 1 SECRETS

1. Get to the Point

2. Every One a ⭐

3. 🎻 Tune Up

4. Don't Be a 🐸

5. The ⚙️ Are Different

6. Stretch 🦒 Yourself

7. It Looks Like an 🐘 to Me!

8. The 👽 Observation

9. Crunch 🔨 the Numbers

10. Step Up to the 🎤

Each of the ten secrets has its own chapter with a consistent structure and similar features. You will be given the "secret code" along with its translation. Look for the magnifying glass

symbol. We'll have fun with this, but more than anything, this book is meant to be a useful handbook for improving teaching, learning, and student achievement. Each chapter contains a practical tip that you can implement immediately in your classroom or school. It will be located next to a pointing finger like the one on the right. You will also find a resource section where you can go to learn more about that particular secret. Complete citations for the works mentioned can be found in the bibliography. At the end of each chapter are notes pages for you to record your thoughts as you process the information and consider how to use it.

In addition to this basic structure, there are other features you will find in each chapter. Storytelling is a highly effective and extremely underused educational resource. Stories have the power to teach content, to pass on culture, to raise standards of behavior, and to make us think—all in an engaging and non-threatening way. Somewhere in each chapter you will see this phrase:

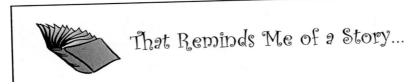

That Reminds Me of a Story...

This lets you know that you can relax a little, put on a smile, and "listen" to a story that makes a point about each secret. These tales come from folklore, literature, urban legend, and personal experience. Sources for the stories are listed near the end of the book.

Reflection—thinking about what we do and why we do it—is rapidly gaining recognition as a means of refining and improving educational practice (York-Barr, Sommers, Ghere & Montie, 2001). Each chapter provides you with at least two opportunities to consider your methods and your beliefs. In a box labeled:

Something to Think About...

you will find an idea or a question, usually directly related to teaching, sometimes humorous, but always designed to be thought-provoking. The second opportunity for reflection is here:

A Word from the Wise...

These quotations are gathered from the worlds of business, entertainment, politics, and education. Whether funny or inspiring, these thoughts provide a slightly different perspective on our attitudes and our choices.

With those tools at our disposal, we are ready to "crack the code" and discover *The 10 Secrets to Higher Student Achievement*.

"Pssst . . . I want to tell you a secret."

SECRET #1:

Get to the Point

Student achievement. It's hard to pick up a newspaper, read a journal article, or attend a school board meeting without encountering the phrase. When election campaigns intensify, politicians utter these words with more frequency and conviction. You would think that educators, if anyone, should know the answer to this question, but just what does "student achievement" mean? The answer is simple. When most people, especially those outside of the field of education, say student achievement, they are talking about only one thing. **The Translation for Secret #1: Student Achievement Means Test Scores.**

We might wonder, why don't people just say what they mean? Well, student achievement certainly sounds nicer, doesn't it? If a political leader said, "I want you to raise your test scores," it could suggest lots of interesting questions:

- Are standardized tests a valid measure of content area knowledge?

- Are there other measures that might be just as valid?

- Are there factors affecting test scores that are out of our control?

- Do standardized tests measure everything we are charged to do?

- Do you want test scores raised at any cost?

These questions have been posed, with little or no response. It seems that, like it or not, our effectiveness will be measured primarily through the results of standardized testing for the foreseeable future. Why?

S omething to T hink A bout...

Standardized tests have been imposed
upon us because we made no effort
to provide a measure of our own effectiveness.

Teaching is a helping profession. Many of us chose education because we felt it as a calling. We work hard. We care about our students. Over the years, more and more demands have been made on schools: special education, drug education, sex education, character education, early childhood education, English language education, and much more. We accepted those added responsibilities, usually without grumbling. And we have done so without a corresponding increase in resources. So, why are we faced with a strident, often mean-spirited cry for accountability?

Education is big business. It is the biggest portion of virtually all state budgets. Local school districts are the largest employers in many communities. We may not like to think of it this way—and the comparison isn't perfect—but the businesses that hire workers and the colleges that admit our graduates are the consumers of our products. They told us for several years that they weren't very happy with the merchandise we sent them. We didn't respond. Horror stories circulated about high school graduates who couldn't read their own diplomas. And so, the testing and accountability movement was born (Popham, 2001).

It would be easy to be bitter about these circumstances, but that would be a mistake. While we may work within the system to change it, for now at least, much of our success will be gauged through student achievement. It is in our best interest to accept that reality and make the most of it. In fact, an alternate translation for Secret #1 is, "Testing is important—so, get over it, already!" That may seem obvious, but we sometimes miss the obvious.

 That Reminds Me of a Story...

The Diamond Mine

Once in South Africa there was a fabulous diamond mine. It was located a mile or two from a small village where most of the workers lived. Because the village was so poor, security at the mine was a serious concern. Each day, the men of the village would rise before the sun, make their way past the gates, and climb down into the hole in the ground. At the end of the day, just before sunset, they walked past guards who carefully searched them for any smuggled jewels. One particular man always got their attention. Each day, he pushed a wheelbarrow full of dirt past them, and each day they searched its contents thoroughly.

Finally, after many years, the man was ready to retire from this grueling work. On his final trip through the gates one of the guards stopped him. "Sir, you have beaten us," he said. "Every day for years you pushed your wheelbarrow by us. We searched it meticulously and never found anything. It's obvious you were up to something. We won't arrest you now, but tell us, how did you make off with the diamonds?"

The old man smiled, "But I wasn't stealing diamonds," he said. "I was stealing wheelbarrows!"

The moral of the story is that—with regard to testing—we need to be aware of our surroundings, focus our efforts, and avoid making assumptions. We have lots of preconceptions about standardized testing, some of them accurate and some not. There are a number of variables in the testing arena; many of them are in our control and some are not. By understanding the difference and using the knowledge of those "secrets" to our advantage, the prospect of improving student achievement becomes much more manageable. Let's see how a captain of industry viewed these sorts of challenges.

A Word from the Wise...

Obstacles are those frightful things you see when you take your eyes off your goals.

—Henry Ford

It has been said that attitudes are contagious. Pet owners know that their animal companions are often very perceptive of human moods and emotions. At home, our own children grow up sensitive to our viewpoints and our values. If it's true of animals and our own children, what about the students in our classrooms? We often underestimate the degree to which children look to us for guidance. That brings us to the **Practical Tip for Secret #1: Check Your Attitude...and If It's Bad, Check It at the Door!** Chances are, the students in your classroom know exactly how you feel about standardized tests. Are you sending the message that tests are a waste of time? Or are they an exciting opportunity to demonstrate what you've accomplished working together? I can't tell you how you feel about testing, but I'll bet your kids can!

TO LEARN MORE ABOUT SECRET #1

Your State Department of Education

The regulation of public schools is the responsibility of each state. While some subject area organizations (like the National Council of the Teachers of Mathematics) have developed what they refer to as national standards, the standards for which educators are accountable have been developed and implemented at the state level. Your state's website should provide you with important information concerning standards and assessment. In fact, most states provide a testing blueprint that describes the relative weight assigned to each of the concepts tested. A listing of links for most of the state departments of education can be found at www.ed.gov/Programs/bastmp/SEA.htm.

The U.S. Department of Education

While the federal government (supposedly) has an indirect role in education, it certainly uses that role to great effect. Traditionally, the federal government provided supplemental funds to help ensure equal opportunity for underserved populations. Recently, the threat of losing those funds has become the "motivation" for implementing federal mandates. Often, as with the recent No Child Left Behind initiative, federal demands are made on states, which pass them on to local districts and schools. You can explore the current federal agenda at www.ed.gov.

Douglas Reeves

A nationally known author, speaker, and consultant, Dr. Reeves has been a champion for the practical implementation of standards. His work has been especially valuable for schools and districts that serve students who traditionally struggle with standardized testing. A pioneer in accountability, Dr. Reeves is known on the Internet as the "Test Doctor." Two of his books that you may want to consider are *Making Standards Work* and *101 Questions & Answers about Standards, Assessment, and Accountability.*

My Reflections . . .

SECRET #2:

Every One a ⭐

"All children can learn."

These simple words first were heard in schools in the early 1980s. They generated controversy then and, consciously or not, educators have been fighting about them ever since. Their reaction often takes the form of questions. What about special ed kids? What about children from disadvantaged families? What about children who don't speak English well? Each of these questions is aimed at the three-letter word at the beginning of the sentence. They express a basic doubt that *all* children can learn.

In order to answer the critics, proponents of this new philosophy began to attach qualifiers and conditions. All children can learn, they said:

- at their own levels.
- given enough time.
- with appropriate instruction.
- what we need to teach them.
- skills necessary to survive.
- something.

While some of these additions speak to how schools and classrooms should operate, others merely serve to comfort us when all of our students don't achieve. These qualifiers allow educators to retain belief in the bell curve, a statistical model that some have adopted as a philosophy of education. A few of our students will excel. A large majority will learn reasonably well. But some just won't make it.

 That Reminds Me of a Story...

Lucky Kids

I was once principal of a high school that might best be described as very "teacher-centered." In the faculty lunchroom, you could often hear the phrase, "I taught it, they just didn't learn it."

During my first summer on the job, I read through the booklet of course offerings to understand the school's program. There were lots of prerequisites, especially in the foreign languages. Students couldn't take Spanish II unless they had at least a B in Spanish I; they couldn't take Spanish I unless they had at least a B in English.

This bothered me. I spoke with the foreign language department chair, and later at several meetings of the full department. I tried to explain that, in my opinion, their standards were too low! Credit in a course should mean that a student has the skills to be successful at the next level. They were passing lots of students that they believed could not be successful. After several conversations, they still didn't—or wouldn't—understand.

In my educational administration classes, I learned that leaders have two kinds of power—personal and positional. Personal power is the most effective. People comply because they believe, because they want to. Positional power ("Because I said so!") is based on fear and is never a long-term solution. After a year of reason and persuasion, I had lost my patience. I resorted to positional power.

I edited the course description booklet myself, striking every grade-related prerequisite. If you passed Spanish I, you were welcome in Spanish II. At the end of the first nine weeks, one of the more vocal members of the department entered my office carrying a stack of papers. She threw them on my desk. "I want you to look at those," she snarled.

"OK," I said, "What are they?"

"They're my grades. Look at them."

I looked down the column. This teacher was known for giving low grades, but these were awful. I paused. "Boy, they're not very good are they? I wonder why that is."

"I'll tell you exactly why that is. Those kids you put in my classes are too damn dumb to learn Spanish!"

I thought for a second. "Then those kids are really lucky."

She looked at me in disbelief. "What do you mean 'lucky'?" She almost spat the words.

"Well, they're lucky they weren't born in Mexico. What would they do then?"

Virtually every child in Mexico—or any other country for that matter—learns to speak the language no matter how "damn dumb" they are. The fact that these students hadn't learned to speak Spanish tells us much more about our system than it does about their abilities. Maybe we should take the time to consider the differences between native acquisition of language (a very complex task mastered by nearly all children), and our methods of teaching those skills in schools.

By the way, although we made some wonderful progress at the school, when I left three years later to take another position, this teacher still didn't "get it." But the good news is that she soon left education for the private sector. And she also contributed to our profession by giving us this wonderful story.

We can often learn valuable lessons by examining the approach and practices of other professions. Doctors surely know that all of their patients won't survive certain serious illnesses. They may even know the statistical likelihood that an individual patient  won't be cured. Even so, we expect them to do their very best for each and every patient and to work toward a 100 percent success rate. That should be our goal, too. Which leads to the **Translation for Secret #2: High Expectations, No Excuses.**

Something to Think About...

If we believe that 95 percent of our students will achieve, who gets to decide which students are in the five percent?

The success of all students is an integral part of the standards-based education movement (Reeves, 2002). Many teachers think that if the district's curriculum is aligned to the state standards, what they do in the classroom must, by definition, be standards-based. Not so. The word "standards" describes a set of expectations for learning that *all* of our students should be able to master and demonstrate. This new model changes the focus in our classrooms. Instead of concentrating on effective teaching (what *we* do), we need to be most concerned with student learning (what *students* can do). Many educators, leaders, and staff developers fail to take note of this not-so-subtle difference.

This change in focus requires educators to do things differently. One of those changes provides us with the **Practical Tip for Secret #2: Develop a Tracking System**. In a standards-based classroom, the teacher must measure, monitor and record the progress of every student. Without a system, that task could be overwhelming. In fact, with an overly cumbersome system, it could be overwhelming as well. Here is very simple model for recording individual progress toward kindergarten standards in mathematics.

Math Performance Objectives for Kindergarten

Class Names	1M-R1 PO 1	Count 1–30	1M-R1 PO2	1st – 5th	1M-R2 PO1	1:1/0–20	1M-R3 PO1 & 1M-R4 PO1	Sets 0–20	1M-R3 PO 2	More or less	1M-R3 P0 3 & 4	+/-; Story Problems 0–5	1M-R4 PO 2	# Names 0–5	Write in Order	0–10

Down the left side are the names of the students in the class. Across the top are the performance objectives from the district curriculum or state standards, with a brief description of each. Progress can be recorded with check marks, pluses, minuses, and zeros, or any other system one might devise. Another method might involve describing more specifically a student's performance relative to each standard. For instance:

E	=	Exceeds the standard
M	=	Meets the standard
A	=	Approaches the standard
F	=	Falls far below the standard

Aside from being a valuable tool for instruction, this very explicit way of monitoring each child's learning reinforces the principle that all children can and will learn. Notice there is no place to record IQ, race, native language or family income. It is implied that every student will make progress toward and meet the standards. Every one a star—high expectations, no excuses.

A Word from the Wise...

So often we wallow in our children's problems rather than exult in their strengths and possibilities.

—Mariän Wright Edelman

TO LEARN MORE ABOUT SECRET #2

The Effective Schools Research

In the 1970s, Larry Lezotte, Ron Edmonds, and Wilbur Brookover conducted the original research on effective schools. They studied the common characteristics of schools that provided quality education with equity for all students. Dr. Lezotte continues the work, updating the research and interpreting it for a new generation of educators. His recent book, *Learning for All*, is a must-read for those interested in academic success for all students.

Educating Everybody's Children

This book, published by the Association for Supervision and Curriculum Development, is designed to provide strategies for teaching our increasingly diverse student population. The components of the Three-High Achievement Model are high-level content, high expectations, and a highly supportive environment. The work continues in *More Strategies for Educating Everybody's Children*.

Ruby Payne

In her book, *A Framework for Understanding Poverty*, Ruby Payne describes some of the differences in worldview and value systems between economic subcultures in our society. She goes on to apply her ideas for classroom teachers. While criticized by some sociologists as simplistic, her ideas ring true for those who work with children from disadvantaged backgrounds.

My Reflections . . .

_____

_____

_____

_____

_____

_____

_____

_____

_____

_____

_____

_____

_____

_____

_____

_____

_____

_____

.

SECRET #3:

Tune Up

A Word from the Wise...

Keep the main thing the main thing.

—Carol Johnson

We hear a lot about curriculum—district curriculum, curriculum alignment, curriculum mapping, curriculum integration, and much more. But just what exactly *is* curriculum? Books, dissertations, and even careers have been devoted to answering that question. If we look across all of this work, we can identify four ways that curriculum leaders have defined the term. (Wiles, 1999) We can see curriculum as:

- A collection of knowledge within a subject,

- A plan for classroom instruction,

- A series of experiences to be provided for students, or

- A set of outcomes or observable changes in students' behavior.

Still, many educators have difficulty in drawing a clear line between curriculum and instruction. Here is a concept that may be helpful: *Curriculum* is what we teach; *instruction* is how we teach it.

Fenwick English, a nationally known curriculum expert, has taken this idea a step further. He says that we don't actually have just one curriculum in our schools, but three distinct curricula (English, 1999). They are:

The WRITTEN Curriculum – What the district believes is being taught. This is what's in that three-ring binder on your shelf that you take down every five years or so to change the pages.

The TAUGHT Curriculum – This is what's <u>really</u> going on in the classroom. What the teachers teach every day, when no one is watching.

The TESTED Curriculum – This is what the state believes should be taught in the classroom. If aligned properly, this content is reflected in the both the state standards and in the state's testing program.

The relationships of these three curricula can be illustrated in a Venn diagram.

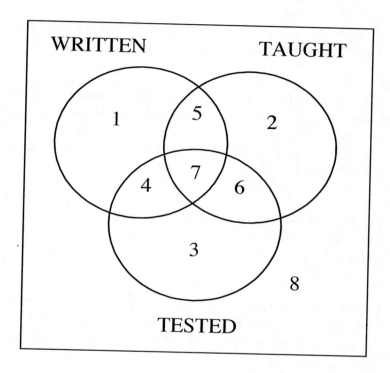

Since this is a typical 3-circle Venn diagram, an individual piece of classroom content might fall into any one of eight areas. Let's take a look at each.

1. **In the written curriculum, but never taught or tested.** Things fall in this area when the district curriculum is not aligned to the state standards and teachers don't see the relevance of the curriculum document. Basically, a waste of paper.

2. **Taught, but not in the written curriculum and not tested.** Material is found here for two reasons. First, the teacher may be "winging it," teaching what she has always taught or what she most enjoys. On the other hand, this is where we often find the "teachable moment." On September 11, 2001, much of what was going on in American classrooms probably fell into this section—and it should have.

3. **Tested, but not in the written curriculum and never taught**. This is bad . . . very bad. If there is much content in this area, students will only demonstrate mastery of the material if they are lucky—in choosing their parents or guessing at answers.

4. **In the written curriculum and tested, but never taught**. This usually means that, for whatever reason, the teacher does not see the curriculum as a useful tool for instruction.

5. **In the written curriculum and taught, but not tested.** If material is found in this section it can be good or bad. If the district has decided that there are things that students should know and be able to do that have been omitted from the standards, this is where they would be found. However, this is also where you would find content taught from a district curriculum that had not been properly aligned to state standards.

6. **Taught and tested, but not in the written curriculum.** This happens either by accident or because the teacher is familiar with the standards and knows the shortcomings of the district curriculum document.

7. **In the written curriculum, taught, and tested.** If you have ever played golf, baseball, or tennis, you may have heard the term "sweet spot." It's that area of the club, bat, or racquet that can knock the ball a mile. The area where all three circles overlap is the curriculum "sweet spot." The efforts of the state, the district, and the teacher have all converged, resulting in the greatest chance for high student achievement.

8. **Not in the written, taught, or tested curricula.** Perhaps time spent talking with students about classroom management might fall in this area, but in general, you should ask yourself, "What am I doing out here?"

While these three circles will never be precisely on top of each other (and probably shouldn't be), we should strive to bring them together as much as possible. In general, it is the district's responsibility to ensure substantial overlap of the written and  tested curricula by aligning the district's curriculum document with the state standards. (We'll assume that the state has made sure that the standards and state assessments are in line.) Once those two circles converge, it becomes the teacher's responsibility to bring her circle on top of the other two: to teach the curriculum and the standards. That is the **Translation for Secret #2: Bring the Circles Together.**

Implementing curriculum in the classroom is not a highlight of most teacher preparation programs. We may have studied the major trends in curriculum design or have spent some time writing behavioral objectives, but we were not often encouraged to identify clear, measurable targets to guide instruction and determine success.

The Archer

A hunter was making his way through the forest, looking for game. He carried his bow and arrow carefully, ready to take aim at the slightest movement. As he stepped into a clearing, he couldn't believe his eyes. On every tree was painted a white target; on some trees there were more than one. And in the center of every target, right in the bull's eye, was an arrow.

As the bowman looked around the clearing, he spied a little cabin over in a dark corner. His curiosity now had the better of him. He walked up to the cabin door and knocked. After a while, the door creaked open very slowly. There in the shadows was a little, shriveled old man. "May I help you?" he asked.

The hunter felt more sure of himself now. "Sir, I'd like to meet the incredible marksman who shot these arrows."

The old man answered, "That would be me."

"Really, sir?" The hunter was skeptical. "Would you mind demonstrating for me? I'd love to learn from your technique."

The old man disappeared into the shadows of the cabin. He emerged carrying a bow and a quiver of arrows. The hunter smiled and thought, "That bow is almost taller than he is!"

In the center of the clearing the old man slowly pulled out a single arrow and laid the quiver on the ground. Shaking slightly, he pulled back the bowstring with all his might and let the arrow fly. It stuck solidly in a tree on the other side of the clearing. Then he went back to the porch of his little cabin, picked up a brush and a bucket of paint, and carefully drew a target around the arrow.

Educators have never been keen on attempts to quantify results. We work with individuals in a social profession. The diversity of their abilities and needs can be overwhelming. Public education requires us to attempt to educate <u>all</u> children. "Quality control" comparisons with manufacturing, where all of the raw materials and conditions can be regulated, are misleading and offensive to us. We are resistant to the use of quantitative measures to describe what, to us, is a qualitative process. But this resistance creates a dilemma. True, no one can say we've failed if our goals are ambiguous. In fact, most of us don't believe we ever fail. On the other hand, without clear targets, we can never know to what extent we've truly succeeded.

One of the most important recent developments in curriculum was proposed by Grant Wiggins and Jay McTighe in their book

Understanding by Design (1998). Their model provides us with a structure for setting clear, measurable targets and offers guidance for reaching them. The three steps they describe are illustrated below.

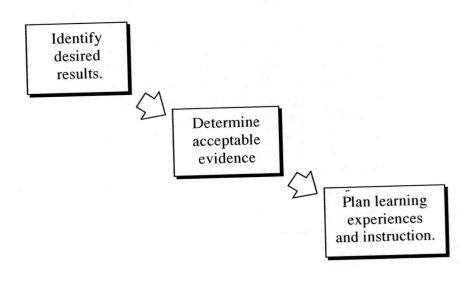

In other words, first we establish exactly what students should know, understand, and be able to do. The next step is to determine what measurements will demonstrate that students have achieved those goals. Finally, we can design classroom activities that will lead students toward the learning targets. This model also provides us with the **Practical Tip for Secret #3: Plan Backwards**.

To appreciate why the *Understanding by Design* model is called backward planning, we can look at the beginning of a typical teacher's career—my own. First, I looked at the textbook. I'd like to say that I consulted the district curriculum, but that would be a lie. Then I planned the lessons for the next two weeks or so, focusing on what *I* would be doing. At the end of the unit, I would sit down—usually the night before the test—and decide what I thought the students should know based on what I had taught. Then the kids would take the test and we'd see where the targets really were. Planning backwards, we ask these three questions:

- What is worth knowing?
- What is acceptable proof that students have gained that knowledge?
- What experiences will help them demonstrate that proficiency?

Something to Think About...

If we don't know where we're going,
how will we know when we get there?

TO LEARN MORE ABOUT SECRET #3

Fenwick English

Throughout his career, Dr. English has been at the forefront of thought on curriculum development and organization. One of his recent works is *Deciding What to Teach and Test: Developing, Aligning, and Auditing the Curriculum.* His concept of the "three curricula" existing in our schools and classrooms resonates with teachers.

Understanding by Design

This book by Grant Wiggins and Jay McTighe has been described as "a landmark achievement [that] has influenced thinkers, writers, and practitioners throughout the world" (Ainsworth, 2003). Wiggins and McTighe have taken the boredom out of curriculum development, making it vibrant and relevant for students and teachers. While grounded solidly in research, their model is practical and accessible.

Unwrapping the Standards

Larry Ainsworth subtitles his book *A Simple Process to Make Standards Manageable*. While state standards can seem intimidating and overwhelming, Ainsworth guides the reader through a process to translate standards into measurable learning outcomes. He then describes how to integrate these concepts with the *Understanding by Design* model for effective classroom instruction. This book is both useful and thought-provoking.

My Reflections . . .

_____

_____

_____

_____

_____

_____

_____

_____

_____

_____

_____

_____

_____

_____

_____

_____

_____

_____

SECRET #4:

Don't Be a 🐵

Teachers like school. In fact, we like it so well we never left! Most of us have been in school, one way or the other, since we were five years old. The structure of school makes sense to us. We've been very successful in this model. The schedule, the rules, and the stability tend to be comforting for us. We have an interest in protecting the institution and its practices. In general, we don't want it to change. This could be our motto:

Something to Think About...

The only person who likes change
is a wet baby!

Needless to say, this attitude isn't very conducive to progress and school improvement. One of the conditions we cling to most persistently is the way we budget and use time. Why does the traditional school year last from August to May? Because young people were needed to help on the farm. Is that still true? Of course not. It no longer makes sense educationally or economically, but, with a few daring exceptions, we have held tightly to an outdated agrarian calendar. Why? Because we have built our schedules, instructional practices, and organizational procedures around it. And besides, we've always done it that way!

 That Reminds Me of a Story...

The Five Monkeys

This account describes a scientific experiment. I don't know if it ever happened, but it makes a great story!

In the center of a behavioral laboratory is a large cage with five monkeys inside. In the center of the cage is a set of stairs with a bunch of bananas hanging over it. Got the picture?

Now, every time one of the monkeys starts up the steps to get the bananas, someone working in the lab pours ice-cold water on the other four. Monkeys are pretty smart, and before too long, they understand what's happening. So, when one of the monkeys makes a move toward the stairs, the other four beat the tar out of him. This happens a few times. Before too long, we have a cage with five monkeys, steps leading to a bunch of bananas, and none of the monkeys will try to reach them.

At this point, the lab workers can even put away the cold water—still none of the monkeys will approach the bananas.

Now, the experiment really begins. We take out one of the original monkeys and replace him with a new one. He thinks, "Cool— bananas!" and starts up the steps. Of course, the other monkeys beat the tar out him. This happens a few times—this is not the brightest monkey. He finally realizes, "I don't know why, but I guess we don't do that here!" Remember, at this point, the water has been put away.

We replace another of the original monkeys with a new one. The process happens again, with the first new monkey joining in thumping on the offender with particular enthusiasm.

We continue this process, replacing each of the original monkeys with a new one. Before too long, here's what we have: A cage with five monkeys inside and a set of stairs leading toward a bunch of the bananas. None of the monkeys will go up the steps to get the bananas, and none of them know why!

That brings us to the **Translation for Secret #4: Question Your Practices—Especially Your Use of Time**. While individual  classroom teachers may not have control over the school year calendar or the bell schedule for the day, some blocks of time are within their control. Bell work or a "sponge activity" (a review or cue-setting assignment written on the board) can help to focus attention and get the class started efficiently. Pre-testing and formative assessment can inform instruction so that time is not wasted on concepts students have already mastered. Teaching to the bell at the end of the day or class can also help to maximize time-on-task.

These suggestions are all pretty conventional. Wouldn't it be nice if we could actually extend instruction? If we could capture some additional time beyond the length of the school day? We try to do exactly that assigning homework, usually with mixed success. A more novel approach is described in the **Practical Tip for Secret #4: Start a Club**. Before you conjure up images of funny uniforms and secret handshakes, let's identify exactly the sort of club we're talking about.

The Alhambra School District in central Phoenix, Arizona, has what can be described as a student population with challenging demographics. The district is located in the inner city. Nearly 90 percent of the students qualify for free or reduced lunch. About 65 percent of the students are English Language Learners. Seventy different languages are spoken in students' homes. In spite of these challenges, the district is known for high student achievement. One of the reasons for this success is the Superintendent's Math Achievement Club.

The Club consists of a series of math homework books, one per month during the school year. If a student completes the booklet, has it signed by a parent, and returns it by the due date, he earns a prize (a very inexpensive toy purchased from one of the well-known import companies). If every student in the class submits a completed booklet every month, the class wins a coveted award: an exciting field trip—to the district office! Students meet with the superintendent in his office, tour the print shop, visit the bus garage, dash through the walk-in freezer, and eat a sack lunch. When they return to their schools they write thank-you notes. And business partners pay for it all.

You might say, "But my district doesn't do anything like that." Does it have to be the Superintendent's Club? Of course not. It could be the Principal's Club or even Mrs. Smith's 4th Grade Math Club. The subject doesn't have to be mathematics, either. The possibilities are only limited by your imagination, which is exactly the point: Try new things and question your practices, especially with regard to time.

A Word from the Wise...

There are only two places where time takes precedence over the job to be done: school and prison.

—William Glasser

TO LEARN MORE ABOUT SECRET #4

Benjamin Bloom

Best known for his Taxonomy of Educational Objectives, Bloom is also the father of "mastery learning." This approach, described in his article *The Search for Methods of Group Instruction as Effective as One-to-One Tutoring,* encourages us to develop clear, measurable, and observable performance objectives and to view time as a variable in reaching them.

Susan Kovalik

With her book *ITI (Integrated Thematic Instruction): The Model,* Kovalik provided teachers with a realistic vision for school improvement, grounded solidly in brain research. Kovalik's methods question some of the "givens" in traditional school and classroom organization. She calls her approach "bodybrain-compatible education." *ITI: The Model* is now out of print, but it has been replaced by a new book, *Exceeding Expectations: A User's Guide to Implementing Brain Research in the Classroom,* co-authored by Karen Olsen.

50 Ways to Close the Achievement Gap

While "No Child Left Behind" is included in the published title of this book, the ideas expressed are not tied to any political agenda and go far beyond that legislation. Carolyn J. Downey and a distinguished team of co-authors provide an extensive menu of best practices and research-based tools for helping all students meet standards. They describe 50 strategies organized around "Six Standards for High Performing Schools." Fenwick English (see Secret #3) is a contributing author.

My Reflections . . .

_____

_____

_____

_____

_____

_____

_____

_____

_____

_____

_____

_____

_____

_____

_____

_____

_____

_____

_____

_____

SECRET #5:

The  Are Different

Something to Think About...

What is the difference between
a farmer and a gardener?

Before you read further, take a few minutes and consider the
question above. Record your thoughts on the next page.

FARMER | GARDENER

Typically, people make some of these points:

- A farmer's field is much larger than a garden plot.

- Farming is a job; gardening is an avocation.

- Most farmers use machinery; gardening is usually done by hand.

- A farmer's goal is uniformity; a gardener values variety.

- Farming is scientific; gardening is artistic.

- A farmer interacts with a field; the gardener interacts with the plant.

Traditional classroom instruction is very much like farming. The underlying assumption is that students are very much alike in ability and development. All of the students get the same lesson, taught in the same way, for the same length of time, and are assessed uniformly. Not surprisingly, the result is a bell curve, that reflects student ability much more than the teacher's intervention. We all know that students come to us with varying experiences, interests, talents, and abilities. In light of that, our classrooms should be more like gardens than farms. **The Translation for Secret #5: All Students Can Learn...But Not on the Same Day and Not in the Same Way.**

Please note that this does not contradict the thoughts presented in Chapter Two. The qualifiers to "All children can learn" discussed in that chapter limited *who* would learn or *what* they would learn. That type of condition usually serves to justify the failure of some students and to relieve educators of responsibility. The Translation for Secret #5 modifies only *when* and *how* the learning will occur. We are not relieved of any of the accountability, but we do get some guidance about how we can accomplish our goals.

Recent educational thought recognizes the need to differentiate instruction. Howard Gardner's work (1983) in multiple intelligences describes the need to appeal to the strengths of individual learners. Brain research encourages us to look at the similarities and differences in the way young people learn (Wolfe, 2001). Much of the work on integrated thematic instruction recognizes the varying interests of children (Kovalik & Olsen, 2002). Carol Ann Tomlinson (1999) pulls together these thoughts and more in her work on the differentiated classroom.

Applying this research on a daily basis is quite another matter, however. The thought of developing thirty separate lesson plans to meet the needs of each individual student seems overwhelming, if not impossible. Beyond that, an individualized approach seems so "soft." In an age of standards and accountability, aren't we always told to be more scientifically based? Doesn't there need to be some consistent measure of progress in the classroom? Even if we're differentiating, shouldn't we be using data to make instructional decisions? The answer to all of these questions is, of course, yes.

Which brings us to the **Practical Tip for Secret #5: Diagnose and Prescribe with Periodic Assessments.** Assessments fall into two large categories, formative and summative, depending upon how they are used. Summative assessments are administered at the conclusion of a lesson, unit, or course of study to determine to what extent the student has mastered a body of knowledge or a set of skills. It serves as a summary of learning. We might also call it "assessment as autopsy." The patient is dead; we just want to know what killed him. Traditionally, we have done lots of summative assessment.

Formative assessment is an integral part of a standards based instructional process. It provides information to shape and form our planning and teaching. Instead of an autopsy, formative assessment is a tool for diagnosis and intervention. Traditionally, we haven't been as consistent in our use and application of formative assessment. Administering periodic assessments, which measure a set of agreed-upon standards at regular checkpoints in the school year, can give us a snapshot of student achievement. This data can guide us in identifying which students have mastered content, which require additional assistance, and their particular areas of need. It provides a foundation for the differentiation that should then occur in the classroom.

The first step in developing periodic assessments is to determine the set of agreed-upon standards. This can happen at the district, school, grade, or classroom level. Using the district curriculum or state standards, teachers determine what content might reasonably be taught in a given time period, often by quarter. As you identify these standards, it is important to consider when standardized testing will occur. Ideally, those concepts best measured through standardized testing should be taught before the testing window. Learning measured through classroom assessment can occur later. These sets of expectations for teaching and learning for each quarter (or other time period) can serve as pacing guides for instruction.

The thought of this kind of structure makes many experienced teachers bristle. "You mean I'm going to be told exactly what to teach and when to teach it? That's teaching in lockstep. Where's the creativity?" they ask. First, remember that these expectations were agreed upon. Teacher ownership is an important part of the process. Next, this has to happen in the real world. Teachers may require differentiation as well. If a master teacher approaches the principal and says, "I know the district pacing guide lists 'money' as something we teach in the first quarter, but I've developed a wonderful integrated shopping unit that I'd like to do right before the holidays," the principal is likely to agree. If a first-year teacher makes the same request, the principal may say, "Why don't we stick to the pacing guide this year and see how that works." After working through the initial concerns, teachers find pacing guides to be a helpful tool for navigating the standards.

Pacing guides serve as blueprints for creating periodic assessments. These tests are not comprehensive of the entire course or grade level; they only measure the content taught so far. For instance, the first quarter periodic assessment would cover only material on the first quarter pacing guide. The assessment for second quarter would be mostly new material (perhaps two-thirds of the test), along with questions to review first quarter concepts (the other third). By the end of the third quarter about half of the test would cover third quarter standards, with the balance consisting of review (one-fourth of the questions from each of the first and second quarters).

These periodic assessments can provide valuable classroom data. We read and hear a lot about the need for educators to employ "data-driven decision-making." This recommendation implies that teachers have lots of wonderful, standards-based data at their fingertips. Initially, it may be necessary to implement some "decision-driven data-making." As a result, we can use real-time, standardized information concerning individual student performance as a basis for choosing appropriate, differentiated instructional techniques.

A Word from the Wise . . .

We have been unyielding in our strategies and absolutely flexible in our expectations. We need to be unyielding in our expectations and absolutely flexible in our strategies.

— Robert Garmston

Dealing with individual student differences in the classroom can be very challenging. Several traditional classroom practices have been developed to help minimize the differences between students. Tracking, ability grouping, and remedial pullout programs are among them. Unfortunately, research tells us that while these methods may make life easier for the teacher, they can actually hinder student learning (Cole, 1995). On the other hand, most of us entered this profession to make a difference in the lives of young people. How could we do that if all children were exactly the same? Helping a student who is challenged (or challenging) can be especially rewarding. We never know how enriching those differences might be.

 That Reminds Me of a Story...

The Cracked Pot

We have come to take running water very much for granted. We turn on the faucet, and fresh, clear water—hot or cold—is available for cooking, cleaning, or drinking. In many parts of the world, even today, water must be brought from its source for use in the home. It is often carried in large clay pots.

In a small village lived a man who owned two such pots. One was almost new and perfect in every way. The other, older pot was dark and stained and had a long crack running from its top to its base. The crack was so big, in fact, that on the long walk home, the old pot lost nearly half of the water it held.

Each night, when the room was dark and the family asleep, the two pots would talk to one another. They often spoke of the day's events and of the sights and sounds of their journey, but, always, the new pot would brag. "My poor friend," he would begin, "It must be so difficult to be imperfect and to accomplish only half of what you were made for. It must make you feel awful." And it did.

The old pot determined to try its hardest to pull together and be as perfect as its partner. But no matter how hard it struggled, the crack remained, and half of its precious contents trickled to the ground on the long walk home.

One day, the poor cracked pot could stand it no longer. As they neared home, it spoke to man who carried them. "I am so ashamed of myself. I want to apologize to you and your family."

Of course, the man was surprised to hear a clay pot talk, but he was also very curious about what it had said. "Why?" he asked, "What do you have to be ashamed of?"

The old pot sighed. "Every day you carry the two of us to the river. You fill us each to the top. And then, when we get home, my friend is still filled to the brim and I am only half full.

You do all that work, and every day I only deliver half as much water as the new pot. I'm so sorry."

The man turned and looked back down the path. "I always carry you on my left side," he said. "Look back down our trail. What do you see on that side?"

"Wildflowers," mumbled the old pot.

"Look at the colors—yellow, purple, pink, and white. Aren't they beautiful?" asked the water carrier. "And what grows on the other side of the path?"

The pot looked. "Nothing."

The man smiled. "Exactly. Each day, your trickle of water moistens the ground and allows those lovely flowers to grow and bloom. Everyone who walks this path is able to enjoy them. Women from the village pick bouquets to brighten their homes. I could have bought a new pot, but without you being just the way you are, no one would ever have experienced this beauty."

We are all cracked pots. Each of us walks the path of life with a particular set of unique faults. Occasionally, we may compare ourselves to others and feel that we come up short. But rather than being ashamed of our differences, if we acknowledge them and make the most of them, we can each spread our own special gifts along the pathway of life.

TO LEARN MORE ABOUT SECRET #5

Multiple Intelligences

Howard Gardner's innovative model was first set forth in *Frames of Mind: The Theory of Multiple Intelligences* in 1983. Gardner's work has much in common with Bloom's Taxonomy: We all know about it (from teacher training, graduate classes, or in-service programs), and it makes sense to us, but few of us have applied the ideas consistently in our classrooms. More recently, Thomas Armstrong has provided *Multiple Intelligences in the Classroom*, a practical guide for implementation.

Differentiated Instruction

If we are to move every child toward mastery of standards, we must begin addressing their individual needs and differences, rather than teaching to them exclusively as a group. Carol Ann Tomlinson has been a leader in this area. Her book, *The Differentiated Classroom: Responding to the Needs of All Learners,* provides commonsense, classroom-tested advice to teachers and administrators to provide for the varying needs of students. *Marching to Different Drummers* by Pat Burke Guild and Stephen Garger pulls together research on diversity, culture, and styles of teaching and learning.

Brain Research

In the past several years educational researchers and practitioners have embraced the exciting and expanding field of brain research. *A Celebration of Neurons* by Robert Sylwester is a reader-friendly handbook on the brain's basic workings. Pat Wolfe's *Brain Matters* is a wonderful guide for understanding the implications of this research and translating it into classroom practice.

My Reflections . . .

_____

_____

_____

_____

_____

_____

_____

_____

_____

_____

_____

_____

_____

_____

_____

_____

_____

_____

_____

SECRET #6:

Stretch Yourself

Staff development. Professional development. In-service programs. Workshops. Retreats. This training. That training. New idea after new idea. These "opportunities" are presented at staff meetings, mandated in edicts from district offices, advertised in professional publications, distributed in our mailboxes, and even spammed by email. You receive countless announcements of the latest and best in education, until finally you think, "I know what I'm doing! Why don't they just leave me alone and let me teach?"

On the other hand, we often complain that educators are not treated as professionals. We think we should receive the same respect and esteem shown to other professions, such as medicine and law. Yet, individuals in both of those professions are expected to demonstrate continuous growth and development. No one would want to visit a doctor who had not learned anything in the last five years. No one would want to hire a lawyer who had not kept up with the developments in the law. Do those same expectations hold for education? Certainly not universally. Some teachers have 20 years of experience, others have one year of experience 20 times. **The Translation for Secret #6: Be a Lifelong Learner.**

Words from the Wise...

We are what we repeatedly do. Excellence, therefore, is not an act, but a habit.

—Aristotle

and...

Anyone who stops learning is old.

—Henry Ford

In the chapter for Secret #4 (Question Your Practices), we noted that educators are very comfortable with the structure and organization of our schools. Sometimes this comfort fosters inertia. We accept things the way they are and stop looking for improvement. "The current system must be pretty good. After all, it produced us!" That way of thinking can be very limiting.

That Reminds Me of a Story...

The Flea Circus

A hundred years ago, traveling carnivals provided entertainment to small towns across the country. Most carnivals had sideshows and a common feature of the sideshows was a flea circus. The "circus" was a small cardboard box with an open top. Inside, the fleas walked tiny tightropes and jumped on little platforms from one side of the box to the other.

The people in these rural areas—many of whom had no running water—were all too familiar with fleas. For them, the most amazing part of the act was that the little creatures stayed in the box at all. They had seen fleas leap amazing distances and couldn't understand how anyone could teach them to limit their jumps.

You might say the trainer's secret was "clear," because to train his tiny acrobats, he simply placed a pane of glass over the top of the box. After knocking their little heads against the glass a few times, they soon discovered exactly how high they should jump. Soon, the glass could be removed and the fleas' leaps would stay just short of their pre-determined limit.

> *Have our attitudes created any glass ceilings in our classrooms? Or for ourselves?*

There is an abundance of wonderful educational research. In fact, it often seems that there is *too* much. Principals and district leaders provide teachers with reach-based strategies and tools. We read about many new thoughts and innovations in education. It's often hard to know where to begin. It's easy to fall victim of "paralysis by analysis"—being so overwhelmed by considering the many possibilities that we do nothing at all. What we need is focus. **The Practical Tip for Secret #6: Try One New Thing.** Select a new research-based strategy that suits your philosophy, style and subject matter. It should also be consistent with the philosophy of your school and district. Understand the theory behind it. Do it often, consistently, and well. Share the strategy with your principal and ask to have it monitored during observations. Share your experiences with others. When you've mastered that technique, select another. Before long, you'll have a toolbox full of new ideas and the satisfaction of being a true professional and a model of lifelong learning.

Most educators are very good teachers. Our experience can be a valuable guide for us. But to remain effective, we must continue to learn and grow. Remember:

$\mathsf{Something\ to\ Think\ About\ldots}$

Experience is the knowledge
of what used to work.

TO LEARN MORE ABOUT SECRET # 6

Research and Professional Journals

While education journals may have been an important part of our teacher training, we're not often expected to use them to refine our practice. *Educational Leadership*, the journal of the Association for Supervision and Curriculum Development, and *Phi Delta Kappan*, published by Phi Delta Kappa International, are scholarly and accessible. Other specialized publications are written for subject areas and grade levels. You might also explore collections of research, such as the *Handbook of Research on Improving Student Achievement*, edited by Gordon Cawelti, which consists of one-page summaries and practical applications for 101 research-based practices.

The National Staff Development Council

This organization, headed by Dennis Sparks, has been a driving force in the reform of staff development. By developing a set of standards, NSDC has illuminated the fact that traditional approaches often fall short of current needs as educators face new challenges. Among these standards are that staff development should be results-driven, engage teachers, and be job-embedded. Dennis Sparks and Stephanie Hirsch present the foundation for this thinking in *A New Vision for Staff Development*. You can find the standards online at www.nsdc.org.

Robert Marzano

We are not relieved of the responsibility for improving our practice simply because our school or district does not provide a meaningful program of staff development. Instead, we must actively seek out our own sources of professional development. One starting place you might consider is *Classroom Instruction that Works: Research-Based Strategies for Increasing Student*

Achievement by Robert Marzano, Debra Pickering, and Jane Pollock. It describes nine specific strategies that have a statistically significant impact on test scores. Marzano also wrote *What Works in Schools*, but I find the previous book to be more readily applicable for teachers.

Your Colleagues

Teaching has been described as a very lonely and isolated profession. Don't forget to take advantage of the years of experience that your peers can share. The recent movement toward creating professional learning communities in schools recognizes the value of learning from each other. *Educators as Learners* edited by Penelope Wald and Michael Castleberry offers a professional development model that supports educators and families in learning and growing together. Less formally, don't underestimate how much you can learn from lunchroom conversation!

My Reflections . . .

SECRET #7:

It Looks Like an 🐘 to Me!

Educators in most schools have implemented measures to prepare students for standardized testing. Teachers talk to students about the importance of attendance during the testing window and of doing their best. Articles in the school newsletter advise parents to feed children a healthy breakfast and to make sure that they get plenty of rest. Important skills are highlighted during instruction and students are alerted that such content may appear on the state tests. Timed assignments accustom students to the pressure of testing situations. But how closely have we examined the format of the assessments themselves? How conscientiously have we integrated the actual question designs into our everyday instruction?

The following true case study illustrates the point. A Midwestern
state was introducing a new standardized test. A major portion of
the language arts subtest dealt with vocabulary and spelling. The
principal at a local high school was confident that his students'
scores would be good. He had been a member of the school's
English department before assuming the principalship.
Vocabulary was taught in every English classroom every week.
Students learned difficult, challenging, multi-syllabic words.
Teachers dictated the words for students to spell. There might
have been cause for worry in some areas, but on these sections of
the test, at least, the school's students should do very well, the
principal thought.

When the results arrived, the principal and the English teachers
were shocked. While the overall results were acceptable, the
vocabulary and spelling scores were very low. In fact, they were
the poorest of all the subtests! The teachers were inclined to
blame the new test, but the principal was perplexed and decided
to investigate. Examining a parallel version of the test, he made
some interesting discoveries. The vocabulary words on the test
were not the obscure, often archaic words taught in the school's
classes. Instead, they were common, but often misused or
misspelled, everyday words. The format of the spelling test was
of interest, too. Spelling words were not dictated. Either
students were asked to choose which one of four spellings of a

word was correct, or they were asked to choose the misspelled word from a list of different words. None of these methods were used in the school's English classes.

The principal met with the members of the English department and presented his discoveries. The teachers agreed to incorporate these strategies into their teaching and assessment. The following year, the scores improved dramatically and the school was recognized for its achievement and growth.

We may think we are preparing our students for what they will be expected to do on standardized tests, but are we attentive to the details? **The Translation for Secret #7: Pay Attention to the Format.**

 That Reminds Me of a Story...

This story has its origins in the Sufi and Indian traditions. An American poet, John Godfrey Saxe, also published a famous interpretation of the tale.

The Blind Men and the Elephant

Once, in days long ago, six blind men were walking down a dusty road. As they walked, they heard something approaching. "Who goes there?" called one of them.

"Two traders," a voice answered, "taking an elephant to the city."

The blind men were excited, chattering among themselves. They were from a very small village and had never experienced an elephant before.

The first blind man extended his hands and approached the elephant. He walked up to its high, broad side. "Ah," he said. "My friends, an elephant flat and solid. It's very much like a wall."

While they certainly trusted his assessment, each wanted to feel the elephant for himself. The second man approached, walking into the elephant's tusk. "Oh, my! What is this? An elephant is not like a wall at all. It's long, and smooth, and pointed. It's very much like a spear."

The third blind man also walked near the elephant's head, but happened to grab its trunk. "A spear? My friend, I don't understand. An elephant is long, but soft and squirmy — very much like a snake."

The fourth man wrapped his arms firmly around the elephant's leg. "Perhaps you *were* feeling a snake, my friend, because an elephant is large and round and stout. It's very much like a tree."

The fifth man touched the elephant's ear. "I'm not sure what you're talking about. Even the blindest person can tell that an elephant is very much like a fan."

The sixth blind man walked up to the rear of the elephant and grabbed its tail. "My friends," he said, "you're all wrong. An elephant is long and swings around. It is very much like a rope."

The blind men took their leave from the traders and continued their journey. As they walked down the dusty path, they argued loudly. Each man was sure, from his experience, that he understood the "true" nature of the elephant. Each was partly right and yet all were very wrong!

Occasionally, we hear discussions concerning the ethics of "teaching the test" or "teaching to the test." There are two important thoughts to keep in mind. First, if the standards, curriculum, instruction, and assessment are properly aligned (see Secret #3), the content we teach should be reflected, precisely, on state assessments. There should be no surprises. Second, our daily methods of instruction and assessment should prepare students to demonstrate on these tests what they know and are able to do. We should not allow a lack of familiarity with the format of a question to impede our students in demonstrating their knowledge. **The Practical Tip for Secret #7 is Align Your Design.**

Examine parallel versions of the test. Take note of the following:

- What student responses are required: multiple choice, short answer, fill-in-the-blank, extended response?

- What mental processes must students use: knowledge, comprehension, application, analysis, synthesis, evaluation?

- Does the content—vocabulary used, structure, level of difficulty—accurately reflect your classroom?

- What does the test look like? What are its type style and size, page layout, and use of graphics and illustrations?

- Are there any other factors that might confuse students? For example, one common standardized test uses letters for multiple-choice answers that alternate between A-B-C-D-E and F-G-H-J-K for every other question.

By examining assessments at this level of detail and incorporating our discoveries into daily instruction, we can help to ensure that extraneous factors do not prevent our students from demonstrating what they know and are able to do on standardized tests. In other words, don't miss part of the elephant!

A Word from the Wise...

A problem well stated
is a problem half solved.

—Charles F. Kettering

TO LEARN MORE ABOUT SECRET #7

Compendiums or Guides for Standardized Tests

Publishers of most commercially developed tests also print a variety of related publications. Most sell technical manuals that give a description of the types of questions asked and the relative weights of the concepts tested. Interpretation manuals can also provide some clues to test format and content. Some testing companies actually market their own test preparation materials. Become knowledgeable about what support materials are available for any commercially prepared tests administered to your students.

State Department of Education

If your state's assessment is developed specifically for your state, there may not be a wide variety of printed materials available. Many states do provide information on the department of education's website. You may find sample questions, blueprints (documents which tell the number and type of question for each standard, concept, or objective), or other publications for parents, teachers, and students. A listing of links to the websites for most state departments of education can be found at www.ed.gov/Programs/bastmp/SEA.htm.

District Assessments, Classroom Tests and Assignments

Examine the instruments provided by the school and district. Do they prepare students for all of the types of questions they are likely to encounter on high-stakes tests? Look at your own classroom tests and the work you assign. Are you helping to prepare students, not only with the content assessed, but with the format as well?

The Truth About Testing

While this book by W. James Popham presents arguments against the use of standardized testing, his criticism of the construction of questions is enlightening. In particular, the chapter entitled *Confounded Causality* analyzes test problems and points up issues associated with content, clarity, and culture.

My Reflections . . .

_____

_____

_____

_____

_____

_____

_____

_____

_____

_____

_____

_____

_____

_____

_____

_____

_____

_____

SECRET #8:

The

Observation

Something to Think About...

If an alien came to Earth,
he would describe "school" as a place
where young people go to watch old people work.

Common sense tells us that in a learning transaction, the person who is doing the work is doing the learning. Yet, in most classrooms, the teacher is engaged in actively "performing" and the students are passive observers. Harry Wong (1988), popular education speaker and author, puts it another way. He invites us to stand outside the school building at the end of the day. The kids run out, whooping and hollering, bouncing and running, ready for play. The teacher comes dragging out to the parking lot, carrying a load of work, shuffling toward the car and home. The teacher has been working very hard, and the students have been perfectly willing to watch. How can we reverse these roles?

 The answer is the **Translation for Secret #8: Make Kids (and Parents) Partners in Learning.** While parent involvement is important, this chapter will focus on how to improve the teacher-student interaction.

Part of the answer lies in brain research (Jensen, 1998). Each day, we are bombarded with millions of sensory stimuli. Without some method of filtering, sorting, and processing these stimuli, we would be overwhelmed. When the brain is confronted with information from the outside world, it asks two questions:

1. *How does this fit with what I already know?*
2. *Am I likely to ever need this information again?*

Through the answers to those questions, the brain is looking for relevance. If the information is found to be important or of interest, it is processed and stored. If not, it passes through, discounted and forgotten.

The degree to which students interact with classroom instruction is called engagement. Phillip Schlechty (2002) describes five levels of student engagement—responses to assigned work—that can be observed in most classrooms:

- **Authentic Engagement** – "This assignment is interesting. It makes sense to me. I might actually use this information sometime."

- **Ritual Engagement** – "I like school. I'm not sure why we're doing this, but I need to get a good grade if I want to go to college."

- **Passive Compliance** – "I'll do your assignment, OK? Don't send me to the office, don't call my mom. I'll do it."

- **Retreatism** – "Just leave me alone. I don't get this stuff and I'm not going to do the work, but I won't bother anybody."

- **Rebellion** – "This stinks. Not only am I not going to do your silly assignment, but I'm going to do everything I can to make sure nobody does it."

When students find content to be personally relevant, they become authentically engaged. This personal connection is a critical component of effective instruction.

 That Reminds Me of <u>Two</u> Stories...

Here are two stories about technology that seem to have conflicting messages. Can you reconcile them?

The Power of the Personal

Electricity had come to the village!

After centuries of living a very traditional lifestyle, the residents of a remote West African community were going to be introduced to the conveniences of the modern world: electric lights, appliances, and of course, television.

When workmen arrived to begin the project, they discovered the village storyteller sitting on a stool in the center of the village, telling stories to the people. Over the next few days, as the wires were connected, the townsfolk were fascinated by the marvels they witnessed. They played with light switches, warmed their hands next to toaster ovens, and pushed their faces close to cooling fans. As the workmen left, they looked at each other and smiled. The people were gathered in the center of the village for stories, but now a TV sat on the center stool, the moving pictures holding the attention of all.

A few weeks later one of the workmen needed to return to the village to make a repair. As he drove his jeep toward the clearing, he couldn't believe what he saw. The television was sitting off to the side, unplugged, and the storyteller had regained his position in the center of the circle.

The workman tapped a young boy on the shoulder. "Is the television broken?" he asked quietly.

The boy, irritated at having his attention diverted at a crucial part of the plot, answered, "No," without turning around.

The workman persisted, "But then why are you listening to the storyteller? The television knows many more stories."

The little boy turned his head and smiled. "That's true," he answered, "But the storyteller knows me."

Bonus Story!

A low achieving, inner-city school had been chosen for a major technology project— computers in every classroom, wireless connectivity, the works. After just one semester, some of the student gains were remarkable. A team of researchers decided to pay the school a visit to determine the reasons for this miraculous progress.

Reviewing the records, they noticed that the gains among special education students had been especially high. A researcher stopped by a classroom, a sat down next to one of the students. This boy had everything going against him. He lived in a dysfunctional home, had a learning disability, and was shunned by most of the other kids. Looking over the files, the researcher discovered that, in spite of these many handicaps, this boy had made incredible gains in mathematics and reading. The researcher asked him what had made the difference.

After a few seconds, the young man replied quietly, "The kids here call me retard...but the computer calls me Raymond."

How do we help to make our classrooms more personally relevant and engaging? One answer can be found in the **Practical Tip for Secret #8: Plan from the Other Side of the Desk.** When most of us develop lesson plans, we plan *our* time—what we will do during the class period. Since we know that the person doing the work is doing the learning, try planning from the student's perspective. Armed with the teacher's knowledge of what is to be learned and how it will be measured (see Secret #3), determine—from the student's point-of-view—which activities and experiences will help you get there. One thing is certain: If you're planning from the student side of the desk, you probably won't say, "I'll walk in to the classroom, sit down, and listen to the teacher talk for 50 minutes." This method of lesson design helps to ensure that we keep our students authentically engaged and actively involved in their own learning.

Finally, this chapter ends with a challenge. On the last page
you'll find a sign for your classroom. The challenge is to hang it
near your desk—and mean it!

TO LEARN MORE ABOUT SECRET #8

Working on the Work

This book by Phillip Schlechty presents a strong case for
providing student work that is relevant and engaging. Schlechty
says there are three ways to improve student performance: work
on the students, work on the teachers, or work on the work that
teachers give students. We have traditionally tried the first two
approaches, with mixed results. Schlechty identifies twelve
characteristics that are present in classrooms and schools in
which work engages students and enables them to learn what they
need to know to succeed in the world.

Inspiring Active Learning

Merrill Harmin has gathered practical strategies used by
successful teachers to help students become active and
responsible learners. A major theme involves creating a
classroom culture that is respectful, collaborative, and supportive.

The book presents 81 separate strategies, each including a description and purpose, followed by insights for its use and implementation.

Classroom Strategies for Interactive Learning

This book by Doug Buehl focuses on middle school and high school levels. It provides 45 literacy skill-building strategies. While grounded in the teaching of reading, the ideas can be easily adapted to other subject areas. The suggestions are research-based, but readable and down-to-earth. A "Strategy Index" shows at a glance the particular skills taught or reinforced with each tool

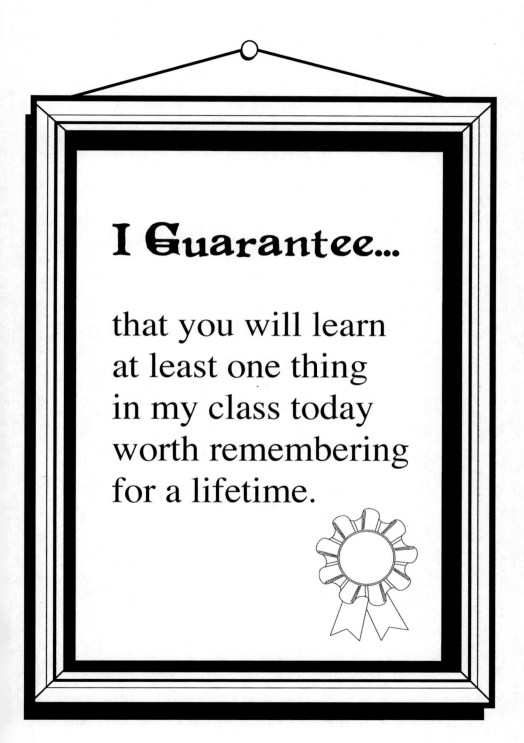

I Guarantee...

that you will learn
at least one thing
in my class today
worth remembering
for a lifetime.

My Reflections . . .

_____

_____

_____

_____

_____

_____

_____

_____

_____

_____

_____

_____

_____

_____

_____

_____

_____

_____

SECRET #9:

Crunch the Numbers

What is the difference between a norm-referenced test and a criterion-referenced test?

The question may be familiar. It could well have appeared on the final exam in a testing and measurements class during your teacher preparation program. Most of us memorized what we needed to pass the course and then promptly forgot it, because the material didn't seem relevant. (See Secret #8.) Now that we could actually apply the information, it is long gone from our short-term memories. So, what is the answer to the question above?

Education has long relied upon norm-referenced testing. These tests generate the normal or "bell" curve. A few students will achieve a very low score (falling at the small, left end of the curve), most will do reasonably well (creating the large hump in the middle of the curve), and a few will get high scores (creating the tapering right side). Norm-referenced tests are designed this way. If too many students do well, the test or the scoring scales must be revised, so that the curve is "normal" again. In fact, one might say that norm-referenced tests are not meant to measure learning, but to sort and compare. If you administer one of these tests to your students, and if they are a normally distributed population, you would expect their performance to generate a bell curve. Intended to rank the performance of individual students, the averages of student scores are often used to rank and rate schools and districts.

Criterion-referenced tests make a different comparison. Rather than compare student scores to each other, the scores are evaluated based upon pre-determined standards. Ideally, the teacher and students know these benchmarks well before the test. While only a few students can score well on a norm-referenced test, it is possible for all students to meet the standards of a criterion-referenced test. Actually, it is not only possible, it should be the goal. When criterion-referenced scores are to be used to compare schools and districts, the comparison is based on the percentage of students who met the standard. More and more, states are relying on criterion-referenced testing.

Let's see how this change in testing and reporting can affect schools. These are very small schools (only 10 students!) but the statistics hold with larger populations as well. The first set of diagrams shows the distribution of scores for each school, under the bell-shaped curve of the "normal" population.

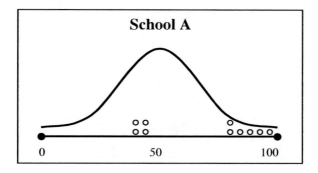

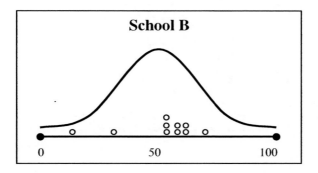

Because this represents a norm-referenced test, we would typically compare the mean (average) of the national percentile scores of the students. The national percentile denotes the percentage of students in the national sample that the student outscored. For School A the mean is 67 (40, 40, 45, 45, 75, 75, 80, 85, 90, and 95, added and divided by 10), very respectable on a national scale. The mean score for School B is 54 (15, 35, 55, 55, 55, 60, 60, 65, 65, 75), slightly above average, but nothing to be too excited about.

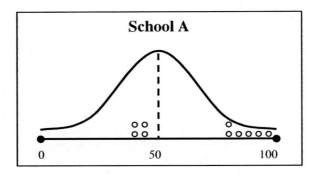

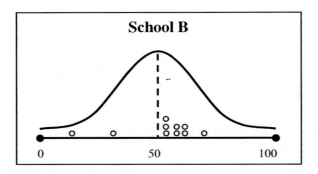

Now, let's say this was a criterion-referenced test and the students earned exactly the same scores. Let's also assume that the arbitrary, agreed upon "passing line" was the same score that would have placed a student at the 50th percentile on the norm-referenced test. To compare the two schools, we would look at the percentage of students who met or exceeded that standard. School A, our high achieving norm-referenced school had 6 students above the line and 4 below, so 60% of its students "passed" or met the standard. School B, which didn't fare as well in the norm-referenced world, had 8 students above the line and 2 below for an 80% passing rate. In a simple criterion-referenced reporting system, School B outperformed School A.

We could argue about which school actually had the higher student achievement, but the point is that we need to understand the basic statistics of the measuring system. Also note that whenever statistics are averaged, information is lost. One of the most common ways we use averaging is in the computation of grades. Which bring us to the **Translation for Secret #9: Become a Statistician.**

 That Reminds Me of a Story...

Fright School

Imagine you are about to begin a cross-county flight on a brand new airline. As you settle into your seat and buckle your seatbelt, the captain's voice comes over the loudspeaker.

"Ladies and gentlemen," he says with an air of confidence, "Not only are you flying on a brand new airline, but you have a brand new pilot as well. I just finished flight school and you'll be happy to know that I graduated with a B average. You're in good hands. Relax and have a wonderful trip."

"Well," you think, "An A average would have been nice, but maintaining a B average in flight school is pretty good. We should be just fine."

And you get comfortable with a new book for your long flight.

Before you get too comfortable though, you might want to know this. The pilot did, in fact, have a B average in flight school. Here's his final report card:

Take-Offs	**A**
Flying	**A**
Landing	**F**

Now what do you think? Are you still comfortable with our pilot? Is a B average still "pretty good?" Does this story have any implications for our grading policies?

Why do we give grades? We want to report student progress and learning. Parents expect them. And besides, we've always done it that way! But are we really sure what those numbers and letters mean? **The Practical Tip for Secret #9: Examine Your Grading.** Rather than asking why we grade, perhaps a better question is—

The flight school story demonstrated the perils of averaging grades. In a traditional system, the same thing could happen in an academic class. A student might score very well on several concepts, have big gaps in other areas, and still be assigned a very respectable grade. This can be a real problem if the concepts the student has not mastered are important prerequisites for learning at the next level. Some districts are developing standards-based reporting systems which show mastery of specific skills, often accompanied by a comprehensive, traditional grade.

Of course, the grades you give students include tests, quizzes, homework, and projects, but do any other factors play a part in your classroom grading system? Do you deduct points for late assignments, forgetting a pencil, or tardiness? Have you ever awarded extra credit for doing a creative project, completing extra homework, or attending a school concert, play, or other event? The more of these practices we employ, the further our grades get from reporting learning. There are certainly student behaviors which should be rewarded and others which should result in negative consequences, but that should happen apart from measuring, recording, and reporting learning outcomes—if that is truly the purpose and message of our grades.

A Word from the Wise . . .

Statistics are like a bikini. What they reveal is suggestive, but what they conceal is vital.
— Scotty Brown

TO LEARN MORE ABOUT SECRET #9

Transforming Classroom Grading

This book by Robert Marzano presents workable alternatives to traditional classroom grading. It emphasizes designing systems that are accurate, precise, and efficient. After presenting the history, theory, and purposes of grading, Marzano discusses seven types of assessment and how they can be combined to form a more honest picture of student performance. Alternatives to traditional report cards are presented, along with strategies for implementing them.

Testing Reports and Interpretation Manuals

Most standardized tests provide materials to help parents and teachers interpret results. Reviewing them can refresh our understanding of what the scores actually mean and how they can help us to guide instruction.

Your State Education Department

Statistics are an integral part of state accountability systems. To the extent possible, understand the formulas for labeling schools and districts and the factors that are included. While I was helping the faculty members of an "underperforming" elementary school understand their state's formula, we discovered that if one more 3rd grader had met standards, they would have received a "passing" designation! It really brought home the importance of helping <u>every</u> child succeed.

School and District Policies

Before you make any radical changes to your own grading system, be sure that your ideas are within school and district policy guidelines.

My Reflections . . .

_____

_____

_____

_____

_____

_____

_____

_____

_____

_____

_____

_____

_____

_____

_____

_____

_____

_____

The 10 Secrets to Higher Student Achievement

SECRET #10:

Step Up
to the

Something to Think About...

Kids will have fun.
It's in their nature.
You can plan for it, structure it, and be a part of it.

Or they will have it at your expense!

A classroom is a community. It has a climate, a culture, and a set of standards for behavior. While organization, procedures, and behavior management are crucial to any well-run classroom, it is very easy to focus on the structures and forget that education is a social endeavor. Each day in the classroom, a teacher has hundreds, if not thousands, of interactions with other human beings. For better or worse, shared experiences create culture. If these mutual experiences are positive, they help to create a safe, supportive community, where the members draw strength from each other (Harmin, 1994).

 That Reminds Me of a Story...

Sticking Together

The old king was dying. Lying in his great, high bed, he could feel his life slipping away. But there was something that troubled his heart even more than his approaching death. His three sons would not stop quarreling. Each thought that he was the stronger and wiser, and should succeed his father as ruler of the land. This had gone on for quite some time, but as the king's strength ebbed, their rivalry grew stronger. The king worried greatly about what would become of them after he was gone.

On the last day of his life, the king called his sons to his bedside. He gestured for his oldest son to come close and whispered in his ear. "Bring me a bundle of sticks," he said. Although they fought among themselves, the sons respected their father. The oldest went to do as he was asked and soon returned with a bundle of small branches, tied together with string.

"I know that you are all anxious to be king," the old man said. "Certainly, this honor should go to the strongest of you. Whoever breaks this bundle of sticks shall be the next king." One by one, the king's sons tried to break the pack of twigs. Struggle as they might, none of them could do it.

"Then let's try this," the king said softly. "Each of you take one stick from the bundle and see if you can break it."

Snap…snap…snap. The three pieces of dry wood splintered.

The old man gathered his strength, sat up in the bed, and looked at his sons. "Taken separately, each of you is as fragile as one of the sticks you broke. But if you work together, helping and supporting one another, you are strong enough to face any challenge."

The three sons looked at each other, ashamed. From that day forward, they never forgot their father's lesson.

And together, they ruled wisely and well.

While the story illustrates that there is strength in numbers, in any community, someone is usually "in charge." In a school community, that person is the principal. Think about the traits that you would like to see in your principal, then consider the following quotation.

A Word from the Wise...

The boss drives his people;
    the leader coaches his.
The boss uses authority; the leader wins goodwill.
The boss keeps them guessing;
    the leader arouses their enthusiasm.
The boss talks about "I"; the leader makes it "we."
The boss makes work drudgery;
    the leader makes work a game.
The boss says, "Go"; the leader says, "Let's go."

—Ted Pollock

Wouldn't it be great to have a principal like that? Perhaps you do. In the same way that the principal is the instructional leader of the school, you are the instructional leader in your classroom. Now read the quotation again. Which traits do students see in your classroom style? Are you the leader or the boss? The **Translation for Secret #10: Model Positive Leadership**, and especially, don't forget to celebrate!

This leads directly to the **Practical Tip for Secret #10: Set a Goal with Your Kids.** The goal you choose could deal with behavior, responsibility, or even student achievement. Some of the skills and traits you can model and teach through shared goal setting include:

- Measurement,
- Computation,
- Estimation,
- Graphing,
- Vocabulary,
- Organization,
- Problem solving,
- Responsibility,
- Cooperation, and
- Anything else you can imagine and incorporate.

By setting goals and working toward them together, we build community and nurture the sense of satisfaction in a job well done. Studies have shown that the ability to defer gratification is important for success. Developing this trait can be an important gift to our students. And it doesn't hurt that it keeps *our* focus on important outcomes as well.

At the end of this chapter, you'll find your own personal "celebration" – a certificate commemorating accomplishment of a goal you set when you opened this book!

TO LEARN MORE ABOUT SECRET #10

Fish!

Based on the operations of the Pike Place Fish Market in Seattle, *Fish! A Remarkable Way to Boost Morale and Improve Results* has become an instant classic in the business and management world. The basic idea is that people are more productive when their workplace has an element of fun. The key principals in the *Fish!* philosophy are to play, to make the day of those around you, to "be there" in your work, and a reminder that we choose our attitudes. The *Fish!* people have recognized that their message could have implications for schools and have created a new division to address the specific needs of educators.

The One Minute Manager¨

Another classic of management literature, this book by Kenneth Blanchard and Spencer Johnson is as appropriate for the classroom as it is the workplace. Dealing with both praise and discipline in a direct, no-nonsense manner not only improves effectiveness, but can actually help build and strengthen relationships. While others have tried to adapt the ideas for teachers, thinking through the educational applications of the original has value in itself.

Books for Inspiration

Recognizing that teaching can be a solitary profession, several authors have written books to provide motivation and encouragement for educators. *Teaching & Joy* by Sornson and Scott is a collection of inspiring stories that remind us how joyful teaching and learning can be. Through stories, poems, plays, and artwork, 42 experienced educators convey the excitement and satisfaction of our profession in *A Passion for Teaching*, edited by Sarah Levine.

The Kids!

Don't forget the enthusiasm for children and learning that led you to teaching in the first place. For some specific ideas, try *Connecting with Students* by Allen Mendler. The book outlines dozens of strategies for bridging the gap between teacher and student through personal, academic, and social connections.

My Reflections . . .

_____

_____

_____

_____

_____

_____

_____

_____

_____

_____

_____

_____

_____

_____

_____

_____

_____

_____

_____

This Certifies that

_____

has Cracked the Code of

The 10 Secrets
to
Higher Student Achievement

and is now Empowered to Deliver
Effective Instruction
and to Share these Secrets with Others.

Awarded this_____ Day of_____,

in the Year 20____.

Jim Garver

Keeper of the Secrets

In Conclusion

So, there you have it. You are now, officially, an initiate into *The 10 Secrets to Higher Student Achievement.* At the very least, you know about ten research-based concepts for improving the likelihood that your students will learn and be able to demonstrate that learning. In addition, you have ten practical tips you can implement immediately in your classroom and a variety of sources to explore for more information. Hopefully, along the way, you have also had the opportunity to examine your core beliefs and your classroom practices.

But, unlike many secrets, these are meant to be shared. Teaching can be such a solitary activity that we are often reluctant to tell others about what we have learned or experienced. Please don't hesitate to reveal these secrets. When professionals share successful techniques, they begin to create a professional learning community, building on each other's accomplishments. Whether you do that is up to you. And, of course...

 That Reminds Me of a Story...

The Oasis

Two travelers were lost in a vast, sandy desert. They had been wandering for many days and were weak from thirst and hunger. In fact, they feared they might die. One of the men looked off in the distance. Could it be? An oasis! He pointed out the discovery to his friend and they ran to get there. One of the men quickly scaled the wall. When he reached the top, he waved for his friend to come and then disappeared on the other side. The other man stood there for a moment, thinking. Then he turned around and walked back toward the desert, determined to help other travelers find their way to this wonderful place.

The End

Sources for the Stories

Good storytellers often take the seeds of stories from other sources, then develop them and make them their own. It is also an accepted professional courtesy among storytellers to acknowledge these sources. While many of the stories related in this book come from personal experience, others have been adapted and expanded. Below is a listing of origins for these stories. While tales were once told around campfires, you will note that many of these stories have come from the campfire of the 21st century, the Internet.

Chapter 1

The story of "The Diamond Mine" has its roots in ancient Turkey and originally was told as part of the exploits of the famous trickster Nasradin. A very early contemporary version can be found in *Good for a Laugh*, a joke book written by Bennett Cerf in 1952. It has since been told and retold in so many contexts that it now qualifies as an urban legend, debunked at www.snopes.com/crime/clever/wheelbarrow.asp.

Chapter 2

"Lucky Kids" is a true story of personal experience. This is its first publication.

Chapter 3

I have heard and read the story of "The Archer" many times. One version appears in *The Best Kept Secret to Achieving Successful School Management* by Carol Grosse and Terri Fields. An online version (that takes itself very seriously) can be found at www.carlopellacani.com/mpo.htm.

Chapter 4

"The Five Monkeys" appeared in my email inbox as one of those anecdotes that gets forwarded to friends and colleagues. As with most of these stories, it had been forwarded so many times that its origins are unclear. One place it has been used is the Motley Fool financial column (www.fool.com/portfolios/rulebreaker/ 1999/rulebreaker991005.htm).

Chapter 5

If you attend religious services, you may have heard "The Cracked Pot" before. It is often used to illustrate the idea that God gives people unique gifts to spread in the world. Entering "cracked pot" into any internet search engine will yield dozens of versions.

Chapter 6

"The Flea Circus" is adapted from a short entry in the May 12, 1992 issue of *Leadership...with a Human Touch*, a monthly publication of The Economics Press, edited by Arthur F. Lenehan.

Chapter 7

The origins of "The Blind Men and the Elephant" are in the religious traditions of the Indian subcontinent. Although it has been told in that context for at least two thousand years, American poet John Godfrey Saxe (1816-1887) composed a famous version in verse. You can find his version in many anthologies and at several sites on the Internet, including www.wordfocus.com/word-act-blindmen.html.

Chapter 8

Both of these stories concerning technology and personalization have been told for several years and have unclear origins. "The Power of the Personal," the tale of the television and the storyteller, can be found (at least in skeletal form) on several web pages, including www.callofstory.org/en/family/language.asp.

The "Bonus Story!" of Raymond and the computer has been used in speeches by Tom Kalinsky, President of Sega America; Dr. John E. Worthen, former President of Ball State University; and David R. Kerwood, Senior Technical Publications Writer and Editor for the Technical Operations Division of the U.S. Naval Undersea Warfare Center.

Chapter 9

"Fright School" is an original story I have told for several years to help teachers understand the limitations of averaging grades (although I'm sure similar thoughts have been expressed by other people at other times). This is its first publication.

Chapter 10

"Sticking Together" is a version of one of Aesop's fables, dating from as early as 600 B.C. It can be found in many anthologies, including *Aesop's Fables* published in 1992, selected and adapted by Jack Zipes.

Conclusion

"The Oasis" is said to have come originally from the Zen tradition. You may find a version online at www.rider.edu/~suler/zenstory/paradise.html, *Zen Stories to Tell Your Neighbors.*

A Word from the Wise...

Most of the quotations in these boxes were taken from *Well Said, Well Spoken: 736 Quotable Quotes for Educators*, edited by Robert D. Ramsey.

References

Ainsworth, L. (2003). *Unwrapping the Standards*. Denver, CO: Advanced Learning Press.

Armstrong, T. (1994). *Multiple Intelligences in the Classroom*. Alexandria, VA: Association for Supervision and Curriculum Development.

Blanchard, K. H., & Johnson, S. (1983). *The One Minute Manager*. New York, NY: William Morrow & Company.

Bloom, B. S. (1984, May). The Search for Methods of Group Instruction as Effective as One-to-One Tutoring. *Educational Leadership*.

Buehl, D. (2001). *Classroom Strategies for Interactive Learning, Second Edition*. Newark, DE: International Reading Association.

Cawelti, G. (1999). *Handbook of Research on Improving Student Achievement, Second Edition*. Arlington, VA: Educational Research Service.

Cole, R. W. (1995). *Educating Everybody's Children*. Alexandria, VA: Association for Supervision and Curriculum Development.

Cole, R. W. (2001). *More Strategies for Educating Everybody's Children*. Alexandria, VA: Association for Supervision and Curriculum Development.

Downey, C. J. (2003). *Leaving No Child Behind: 50 Ways to Close the Achievement Gap*. Johnston, IA: Curriculum Management Systems, Inc.

English, F. W. (1999). *Deciding What to Teach and Test: Developing, Aligning, and Auditing the Curriculum*. Thousand Oaks, CA: SAGE Publications.

Gardner, H. (1983). *Frames of Mind: The Theory of Multiple Intelligences*. New York, NY: Basic Books.

Guild, P. B., & Garger, S. (1998). *Marching to Different Drummers*. Alexandria, VA: Association for Supervision and Curriculum Development.

Harmin, M. (1994). *Inspiring Active Learning: A Handbook for Teachers*. Alexandria, VA: Association for Supervision and Curriculum Development.

Jensen, E. (1998). *Teaching with the Brain in Mind*. Alexandria, VA: Association for Supervision and Curriculum Development.

KFC. (2002). *About KFC: Colonel Sanders*. Retrieved March 18, 2004, from www.kfc.com/about/colonel.htm

Kovalik, S., & Olsen, K. (2002). *Exceeding Expectations, 2nd Edition: A User's Guide to Implementing Brain Research in the Classroom*. Covington, WA: Books for Educators, Inc.

Levine, S. L. (1999). *A Passion for Teaching*. Alexandria, VA: Association for Supervision and Curriculum Development.

Lezotte, L. W. (1997). *Learning for All*. Oskemos, MI: Effective Schools Products, Ltd.

Lundin, S. C., Paul, H., & Christensen, J. (2000). *Fish! A Remarkable Way to Boost Morale and Improve Results*. New York, NY: Hyperion Press.

Marzano, R. J. (2000). *Transforming Classroom Grading*. Alexandria, VA: Association for Supervision and Curriculum Development.

Marzano, R. J., Pickering, D. J., & Pollock, J. E. (2001). *Classroom Instruction that Works: Research-Based Strategies for Increasing Student Achievement*. Alexandria, VA: Association for Supervision and Curriculum Development.

Marzano, R. J. (2003). *What Works in Schools: Translating Research into Action*. Alexandria, VA: Association for Supervision and Curriculum Development.

Mendler, A. N. (2001). *Connecting with Students.* Alexandria, VA: Association for Supervision and Curriculum Development.

Payne, R. K. (2001). *A Framework for Understanding Poverty.* Highlands, TX: Aha! Process, Inc.

Popham, W. J. (2001). *The Truth about Testing: An Educator's Call to Action.* Alexandria, VA: Association for Supervision and Curriculum Development.

Ramsey, R. D. (2001). *Well Said, Well Spoken: 736 Quotable Quotes for Educators.* Thousand Oaks, CA: Corwin Press, Inc.

Reeves, D. B. (2001). *101 Questions & Answers about Standards, Assessment, and Accountability.* Denver, CO: Advanced Learning Press.

Reeves, D. B. (2002). *Making Standards Work.* Denver, CO: Advanced Learning Press.

Schlechty, P. C. (2002). *Working on the Work: An Action Plan for Teachers, Principals, and Superintendents.* San Francisco, CA: Jossey-Bass.

Sornson, R., & Scott, J. (1997). *Teaching & Joy.* Alexandria, VA: Association for Supervision and Curriculum Development.

Sparks, D., & Hirsch, S. (1997). *A New Vision for Staff Development.* Alexandria, VA: Association for Supervision and Curriculum Development.

Sylwester, R. (1995). *A Celebration of Neurons: An Educator's Guide to the Human Brain.* Alexandria, VA: Association for Supervision and Curriculum Development.

Tomlinson, C. A. (1999). *The Differentiated Classroom: Responding to the Needs of All Learners.* Alexandria, VA: Association for Supervision and Curriculum Development.

Wald, P. J., & Castleberry, M. S. (2000). *Educators as Learners: Creating a Professional Learning Community in Your School.*

Alexandria, VA: Association for Supervision and Curriculum Development.

Wiggins, G., & McTighe, J. (1998). *Understanding by Design.* Alexandria, VA: Association for Supervision and Curriculum Development.

Wiles, J. (1999). *Curriculum Essentials: A Resource for Educators.* Needham Heights, MA: Allyn & Bacon.

Wolfe, P. (2001). *Brain Matters: Translating Research into Classroom Practice.* Alexandria, VA: Association for Supervision and Curriculum Development.

Wong, H. (1988). *I Choose to Care* [Videotape]. Mountain View, CA: Harry K. Wong Publications, Inc.

York-Barr, J., Sommers, W. A., Ghere, G. S., & Montie, J. (2001). *Reflective Practice to Improve Schools: An Action Guide for Educators.* Thousand Oaks, CA: Corwin Press, Inc.

Zipes, J. (1992). *Aesop's Fables.* New York, NY: New American Library.